Brink

Poetry collection

Farzana Habib

Ukiyoto Publishing

All global publishing rights are held by

Ukiyoto Publishing

Published in 2022

Content Copyright © Farzana Habib

ISBN 9789360164201

All rights reserved.

No part of this publication may be reproduced, transmitted, or stored in a retrieval system, in any form by any means, electronic, mechanical, photocopying, recording or otherwise, without the prior permission of the publisher.

The moral rights of the author have been asserted.

This is a work of fiction. Names, characters, businesses, places, events, locales, and incidents are either the products of the author's imagination or used in a fictitious manner. Any resemblance to actual persons, living or dead, or actual events is purely coincidental.

This book is sold subject to the condition that it shall not by way of trade or otherwise, be lent, resold, hired out or otherwise circulated, without the publisher's prior consent, in any form of binding or cover other than that in which it is published.

Dedication

This book is dedicated to all the people who are in a bind and facing difficulties while trying to stay sane all at the same time.

The following poems tells stories of people who have been through one ordeal after the other and specifically look into the final moments before they are ready to snap or close to reach their breaking point.

Contents

I love you pumpkin	1
3 days	6
Calling the shots	8
Silence	9
Numb	11
Writer's block	12
Running	13
Out of order	15
Bump	16
Confession	18
The party	19
Circle of fire	21
Going home	23
Failure	25
Lifeline	27
Tired	30
Home maker	32
Why	34
Cursed	36
Feeling low	38
Living in a glass house	40
Always falling short	41
Triggererd	46

| Negative | 47 |
| *About the Author* | *48* |

I love you pumpkin

As they lowered my mother's casket into the ground
I held on to my father's hands tightly
I looked at my father—failing to read him
His grey eyes looked at nothing in particular
And lips uttered words only he understood

He let go of my hands abruptly and started walking ahead
Leaving me behind with my aunt and her husband
I stayed with them till it was time to go home

Home

The word sounded strange to my ears
What good was a home if you did not have a mother to go home to?
One who you could talk to about all your worries
Rest your head on her lap and feel all your tensions drift away every time she stroked your hair

But I had to go anyway—It has been raining and I was soaked to the bone
When I got home
The air smelled musty and everyone was still in their "mourning clothes"
If I had my way I would throw away my Wednesday

Adams inspired frock and Mary Janes into the fire

My family sat around the kitchen table and tried their best not to weep into the food that was sent by the neighbors
I had no appetite to even begin with so I left the table without saying a word
I went to my room changed my clothes and flopped on my bed
I was too tired for anything else and wanted to be left alone for the rest of my days
But this was just wishful thinking

My father had started behaving strangely only a week later
Coming home late into the night and bringing with him empty bottles and strange odors instead of dinner and clothes
Forgetting to restock the fridge and pay the bills on time
I was busy with school but I pitched in to help whenever I could

But nothing ever pleased my father!
"Lola why are the eggs burned" that earned me a pinch on the arm
"Take out the garbage" he would yell out and smack me across the head
"The soup tastes like dishwater"

The complaints increased with time and the beatings as well
There were 7 days in a week and he may be spared me for two
I was changing colors like chameleon from blue to purple and looked more like a rag-doll then a 14 year old girl
I hardly fit into my school uniform anymore

I could not remember how long this went on for but soon enough it was routine
He would beat in the day
And come to my room to sooth my wounds during the night

He never apologized- all he had to say was this "I love you pumpkin"
As if that was enough to heal the cigarette burns he placed on my arms and legs
My bruised face
Purple eyes
Broken bones

Things took a turn for the worse on my 17 birthday
My father would only come home now at night just to slowly creep into my room and check on me
Not on my wounds but my body instead
My eyes remained closed the entire time but that never helped
He was a big man and had me easily pinned to my bed

He slapped me about when I tried to get away and
thrashed around like a fish out of water

He only had this much to say
"I love you pumpkin"

Going to the police did not help
I could not inform my aunt and My grandmother was
buried six feet under the ground

July 1st The day of his birthday
I decided to end this once and for all
At exactly 11 pm
The front door creaked open and I could hear the
sounds of heavy footsteps making their way to the
living room

The lights came on and I got into character
My father was very startled to see me
"Luna" he croaked
The man was drunk
I gingerly embraced him before coaxing him to sit in
my mother chair and busied myself with house chores
After an eternity later I could see he was a little
calmer then before
I continued what I was doing but this time using only
one hand
And reached for the frying pan I had kept hidden out
of sight
Before he could take my mother's name again
I brought the pan down and struck him on the head

I smiled when the blood finally started to trickle down

With a satisfied smirk I only had this much to say "I love you pumpkin."

3 days

I know life goes on and time waits for no one

The moment we are up there is something that needs to be done and sometimes even re-done.

Now what if all that was to come to a halt one day?

Your usual check-up with the family physician turned into something dreary?

He does not welcome you with his usual smile but frowns at you instead

Looks over at the small sheets of papers in his hands and quickly leaves the room

To have an elderly nurse come in and all tell you that your time is short

You have only 3 days on earth

Today is Friday and you expire on a Sunday

The day of rest…

The long lasting feelings of fatigue

Your fine hair thinning out

Hunger, no longer an issue

Thinking that it just stress and sleepless nights responsible for your horrid state.

Your mouth isn't working but hands reach your eyes and to your surprise there are no tears

You don't have time for that either

On your home you think about what you will tell the mother who looks forward to seeing your face first thing in the morning

The father who patiently waits for you to take over the family business so that he could stretch his legs

The baby sister who expects you at her wedding dressed in your finest

And the sweet man who promised you that sleeping alone will soon be a thing of the past

What about your dream?

That childlike wish you held on to for years to become a superhero wearing a stethoscope and handing lollies to all the sick children left and right

Suddenly the path to your house, the same one you grew up in is over

And the heavy oak door opens up

To let out frenzy of noise complete with laughing children and talkative adults

Bessie the friendly black Labrador is there too

You look to the sky and sigh "I guess this can wait till after the party"

Calling the shots

This marks the end of another stressful day
Y'know working for a law firm isn't all that glamorous
and defending woman and children is very draining
It certainly does not help that you are in a room only
two doors away from a man part of your past
the walls and closed doors do nothing to conceal your voice
The voice that told me It was time to see other peoples
what I gave you was not enough
You did not waste any time in socializing
while I stayed back drinking away my pain in liquids
One shot for Valerie my red haired ex best friend
One shot for Ronnie the piano playing colleague at work
One shot for Ashley my cousin the successful lawyer
One shot for Rita the almond skinned doe eyed newbie at work
Let's not forget the pills
cause no martini is complete with an olive or three

Silence

When you showed up at my door with roses and chocolates on my birthday I could not say no

When you proposed to me up in the air on a hot air balloon with a ring bluer then my eyes, I could not say no

When you set me down in front a of a mansion made from glass and crystal which I could fill up with my dreams

I could not say no

When you got busy right after the wedding and buried yourself in your work and stayed out real late

I could not say no

When you picked up the phone sounding half intoxicated with a with a female companion snuggling up to you

I could not say no

When you would cancel all our lunch or dinner plans
and spend them with your friends instead

I could not say no

When you would go out with your pretty little perky
secretaries in the name of business I could say no

When I would ask to come along you could not say
anything

Where did we go wrong?

Numb

I feel it all the time now
Nothing less
Nothing more
I think I prefer it this way

Writer's block

The ivory page with the floral detailing stares back at
me
waiting to be caressed the soft tip of a feather or pen
my array of colored ink and lead lay motionless on the
mahogany desk
There is plenty going through this head of mine
but I am unable to write tonight
A simple sentence, stanza, song or story
the task of jotting down words, and forming
sentences is too much for me
The letters do not flow, they have become scrambled
up like alphabet soup
the sentences make no sense and are falling apart like
my favorite pearl necklace
my voice is broken
The paper void of words, emotion and passion, is
soaking up tears

The red ink has bleed into my fingers

Maybe some things are better left unsaid.

Running

The last 10 days have passed by in a blur
A blur I do not wish to relive
I wake up at nine and am greeted by a scowl
a look of indifference or just a long list of chores
domestic duties
endless errands
messy mundane nonsense
It leaves me aching and miserable at the end of the night
24 hours seem too little now
I feel like I should have my shoes on at all times
perhaps even wear them to bed
Running from one point to another
but it never seems to end
I spend the days doing all kinds of things
but there is little to no room for the things that matter
to me
Sleep
Oh how I miss you!
Homework and studying
I am sorry I have to complete you in a rush or neglect
you for days at a time
Showers
You are either too cold or too fast
simple things but they are usually out of my reach

When will I be able to go home and sleep
Not like the dead
but in sheer peace
feel the prick of slumber slowly inject itself in my mind
and dull my senses for the next 8 hours
Let it consume my overworked brain with dreams
not the ones filled with demons violence and blood
dark as ink
but the ones with with color, laughter, smiles, and bliss
I am just about ready to leave this reality
filled with people I do not want to see
filled with tedious tasks and objectives that test my patience and adds more grey to the red in my hair
filled with unless chatter when my brain screams for silence
golden comforting silence
Be free of pain, loneliness, and overwhelming confusion that has taken over my life
I long to be part of a new world
A new reality
I have already lost control once
Now I fear that I will loose myself completely in this mayhem of madness as well

Out of Order

There are 24 hours in a day but I always have 25 things to do

I am unsure of what to begin with, what to discard and what to leave for tomorrow

The cooking, cleaning, sweeping, moping, serving, redoing, undoing, and bickering is done on a daily basis

Attending class, completing projects and assignments, note-taking, pent up frustration and procrastinating goes happens every other day

My sleeping cycles are irregular

My appetite is hit or miss

My acne is on point

A bad hair day is the norm

Blood shot eyes, short temper and newly found pessimistic behavior is all I ever wear now

Confidence levels are sinking

Anxiety levels are rising

How do I fix this?

A new haircut and coffee I.V?

Get my nails done and put on that and have on that make it till you fake it attitude?

Bump

We tied the knot in May

We have been trying for close to a year

He wants a baby

I am just doing my part

This was definitely not planned

Not for another year or so

I haven't even graduated from college

He hung up his cap and gown a long time ago

I still have a trouble juggling being a Mrs and going to school

Cooking & Reading

Cleaning and Essay Writing

Laundry and Tests

Its terrifying at times and down-right draining

He will be overjoyed by the news

So overcome with emotion that he will not know what to do with himself

I am filled dread, sadness, pity and anger

Dread for the next 9 long months

Sadness over the future that will never be mine
Pity for giving into societal pressure to get married
Angry that everyone else is happy but me
I am tired from all that pacing
of my feet
of my thoughts
My head hurts from all the tears
I cannot find a solution to this
I cannot imagine a world with a miniature version of myself
I cannot go through with this

Confession

I'm sorry we fight so much
Late at night
Sleep deprived
Hungover on old memories and faces
Wishing that it was 1972
Mary's dead and gone
Peter's in rehab
And the baby eloped
I'm sorry I didn't tell you
I don't blame you anymore
I know you tried
working overtime brought in the goods
but we were loosing the kids
Weekly trips to the hair salon and Dairy Queen
made them smile a lot
but it was all out of fear
We should have listened when it was time to be quiet
Give out hugs on the daily instead of beatings
Hold them close instead of locking them indoors

I guess what I am trying to say is that I am sorry

The Party

The clock on the wall reads 11:58 PM

Where are you?
I cannot sit still anymore
pretending that all is well
this party was a bad idea
you insisted so I came
the house has been decorated beautifully for the occasion
the food a tad spicy but delicious
the hostess is so full of grace
28 bright eyed and carefree

I feel like I do not belong
I am cooped up in the parlor
with a group of woman
mid 30's late 40's
all dressed in blue
who I do not wish to ever see again

The one to my right says that she saw you at the pub
necking with her little sister Gwendolyn
the one of the left boasted about all the little trinkets
you bring to her every Thursday

Pay day no?

The one in front of me bringing in colorful drinks
is praising your looks and masculinity

Why do you go out of your way to belittle me
What is it that they posses, that you cannot find in me?

Circle of fire

Everything is going wrong
I am broke with no job prospects coming in
it's hot outside but I feel cold and sick
Bills need to be paid but I don't know if i have
anything worth selling
except for blood and plasma
just graduated but where is my big moment
guess it doesn't exist
the doctor visits are long and endless
did I mention expensive too?
a baby is not guaranteed
the house use to feel very big to me earlier
now I think it's not big enough
to keep him out of my sight
Conversation is pointless when all he gears up for is
confrontation
we are suppose to meet up with family soon
but it's all for show
we wants to go so that he can relax
after complaining to his mother no doubt
I just think I will raise my BP

Everything is going wrong
he is out of the picture as usual
there is hostility everywhere

I think I am too tired to care
or maybe I am the problem
because all I feel
is strangely zen

Going home

It is time to go home

But I do not know who will be greeting me at the door tonight

It is always something different, 7 days a week

On Monday, he comes home overworked and vents about work

On Tuesday he stays home and sulks and because my mom stays with us for the
night every week, after dad passed away not too long ago

On Wednesday he comes exhausted from night school and does not fall asleep before one

On Thursday, He sits in his favorite chair, red faced and wild eyed because he is baby sitting a six year old
S
It is his son as well

On Friday, he is crabby because he his friends cant come over to play

On Saturday, he is not home, because he is out for a night of fun, gossiping, and backbiting

On Sunday, He is home asleep before I even get there.

I am just about ready to give up on him
On us
Walk out that door
Don't ever look back again

Failure

This is our last session to

gether in the same room sitting next to each other
I will walk into a room and witness another piece of my marriage coming undone
My beautiful wife expressing all her anguish and all the emotions she has bottled up for the past 20 something years because life got in the way.
The stress and anxiety surrounding the birth of a new baby.
Walking on eggshells trying to be perfect around the in laws
Feeling drained because of a group of rambunctious cousins and siblings
Nights wasted on hurling nasty words at each other because we were both tired from the lack of sleep, touch, and because we were not listening
Not once did she think about reaching out to me and tell me how she feels
What hurts and what feels good
Take only the briefest moment to let me know that she wanted to take a break from being the best mother, wife and daughter
The superglue that held together out family of four
Protecting it from the dangerous winds full of unkind words and backbiting

Raising two beautiful sons without taking any sick days
Turning an old duplex into the garden of Eden
With her artistic abilities, endless swatches of color and tiny fingers
I miss her handmade handkerchiefs
One for each day of the week
Dipped in lavender and stitched with words from the heart
Words that I never paid any attention too
They have only gathered the results of my hard work
Sweat, tears and on occasion, droplets of blood
From 8am-6pm
I am not a man of even-temperament
But I wonder how she has managed to keep it all together for so long when she was really falling apart
She has the habit of staring into the mirror after a bad quarrel
I have no idea what she keeps looking for
Her skin robbed of a healthy glow
Hair that has more grey then black in it
Lines that were never there before
Did time do all that for was I the reason behind it
I only did what my father taught me
Go to school get a degree, work without breaking my back and provide my family with a life people only dream about
Now I fear that I cannot repair what time has erased for me, my wife, as individuals and as a couple.

Lifeline

He is blessed with all that his parents have provided him with

He did all that he could as the eldest son in the family

But life began when he met her…

She came into his life at '92

March 7th 1992 to be exact

It was all arranged

The elders knew best and the rest was up to them

He though she looked great draped in her fuchsia saree and green eye shadow

Maybe just a little on the thin side though

The wedding wass no special affair

But he knew that he had married a special girl and he was the lucky one

She smiled all the time no matter what the weather was like outside

She always did what as asked of her and much more

She was a team player but quickly won all the hearts in the household

She was quiet and a tad shy but always praise-worthy

She worked tirelessly

Cooked passionately

Love unconditionally

She faced many hardships till now

But did not let her patience waver one bit

Or let time erase any of the hope stored in her heart

For a better future

A brighter tomorrow

Away form unnecessary comparisons between other wives, back biting, complaints and exaggeration

Despite all that she never wiped the smile off her face

As months turned to years it got smaller but never completely faded away

She worked hard at creating a perfect house

Perfecting her cooking and artistic skills

Keeping the peace among other family members

While achieving all of that she also taught him a few things down the road

She taught him how to hold on to his temper when he was about to loose his cool

She taught him how to hold on to his patience when he become anxious and started talking rubbish.

She taught him how to hold hos tongue and swallow his pride

She taught him when to take a step back and when to stop talking

He still has not learnt that one yet!

She paid heed to his words whenever there was no one else to listen to him

She stood beside him when he was lost

He hated asking for directions

Together they spent 25 years together and I hope they get another 50 more

I am not sure how it all passed by

Mom kept it all together

But the house is empty now

Looking neglected and shabby without her touch

The food tastes bland

My father cannot sleep

His cycles have become broken and interrupted

My siblings hide themselves in the comfort of their rooms

Keep busy with school and work

But a locked door is not strong enough to block out the sounds of their muffled cries

We all hope and we all pray

But there is no telling when she will walk through that door and bring life into this house

Please come back soon Mom!

Tired

How are you feeling today he asks

Tired I answer back without moving a muscle

Tired of being stuck in one place

Tired of going to school and unsure of what comes next

Tired of staying married to a man who is always busy

With what?

Not sure

But always busy

Tired of carrying forth a dead relationship

Tired of cleaning a house that will get messy the next day

Tired of his mom, she will be leaving soon but I just want to be alone

Tired of wondering what my future holds, is it bright or endlessly dark?

Tired of attempting to smile when all I want is to stay in bed

Tired of drinking coffee, cup after cup to mask the
obvious signs of fatigue in my face and body

Tired of rubbing my eyes and just hanging on

Uh that's nice he responds staring down at his phone
with his mind millions of miles away from here

From me

Home Maker

It has been exactly one year since you have brought me into this house

Carried me over the threshold and step further

I have turned to this house into a fine home

Looked after your parents like they are my very own

Treasured your sister like the one I never had

I smiled every time you went for work and left me cooped up in the house

I gave it no thought every time you came home and plopped yourself right in front of the TV

I kept quiet when you waved at me from your office because there was always something or someone that always needed your attention

I went about my way every time you asked for the bottle, and never for me

I closed my eyes when you crept into bed at 2 am in the morning thinking that I would not hear anything

But I must say I am tired now

Tired of keeping appearances and pretending to be happy

When really, every part of me wants to lash out
Smash the fine china to decorate the floors
Paint the walls with your imported poison
And make curtains out your clothes
Acknowledge me while I am still here
Look at me when I sit across you
Embrace me— "thud"
That was the door

Why

My mama always said that I was a beautiful baby with light brown hair and curious 'blue eyes
Quiet and obedient as a young boy and studious as a young man
So different from all the other boys... In the world
So I asked her a question one day when she sat down to do her embroidery
Mama why am I So different from all the boys in town?
They are so rowdy loud and always so drunk
She me for a moment and gave my left ear a great tweak
Why George! Your just perfect like your daddy
You have eyes to see with, two ears to hear with and ten fingers and toes to move around and explore the world with
Ah! It was useless trying to explain anything to my dear old mother
The truth was... I did not want to be like daddy!
Having to cut my hair every couple of days when she wore hers down to her shoulders
Always stuck wearing dress shirts and pants in the house when she bounced around in such pretty floral frocks and matching pointy shoes
Being told to do better in school and keep busy with

fixing cars and junk in the house
When she looked so happy baking cakes and pastries,
running errands and waiting for daddy to come home
with his hands filed with flowers and chocolate Bon
bons
Worst of all being told that boys cannot cry
But I'm in pain and always so miserable
So why is it so forbidden for me to cry
Just to shed a tear or two

Cursed

Maybe I'm overthinking this
Or looking for a solution where there is none
I have finally accepted the fact that I am not the one
for your
You for me
You won't realize a thing the day I leave
Maybe it was just melodrama on my part
Or maybe just sadness too
How easy it is for you to meet someone and form
relations
Then break them off at your own whim and
convenience
I curse my self for this
For being who I am
I can talk till your eyes fill
But my actions never measure up after
I apologize even when your wrong
I apologize when my out of line
I am left to feel and weather through the storm of
emotion
One wave after the next as they wash over me
Still expected to be standing in the end
You used to always say that I was soft hearted
Was that a reminder?
An observation

Or something you secretly took pleasure in
When you were all fired up and ready to tear me to pieces
I curse my sake got being who I am
For still not being able to change
I wish I could be as strong and heartless like you

Feeling low

I want to know what makes someone
Especially a man
You never liked me
I tell myself that often as a reminder
I've realized it later then ever
Why not at the beginning
I don't know
Was it because I was hopeful
Was it because I wanted to give you chance after
chance to prove to me that your actually human
That your feelings were actually genuine
That you were selfless
You knew how to love
How to perhaps mend together my broken pieces
But you were just broken
More so then me
Held together by wealth religion and your so called
good deeds and luck
I paid one hell if a price for listening to others
for staying with you even when I should have steered
clear of you
It was like giving shelter to the a helpless pup or
kitten back then
I didn't think you were going to be such a handful
later

I couldn't keep you out of kindness and compassion
Now I wish you would just leave and never come back
You can't stay well
You don't let others stay well either
But you've had your fill of me
Now still hell bent on turning me as lifeless as you

Living in a glass house

I live in one
things break and crash around me all day long
I have been very careful
but all I do is clean up glass
beautiful and fragile to others
painful and frustrating to me
I wish to get out of here
but unable to because everyone thinks
that a glass house is befitting
It's what I deserve and nothing less
here is hoping that everything tumbles down
crashes to the floor and beyond repair
shoes are sturdy
covered from head to toe
so tired of cleaning glass
I would hand over the key in a blink
but no one will take
everyone is afraid of responsibility
while I hate the false glory

Always Falling Short

I am convinced that I am terrible

Otherwise why would I even cross paths with you

It was no godly intervention

The union was borne from greed and grief of many sorts

I didn't like you then

I don't like you now

Not the way I'm suppose to

You asked for my hand

For all the wrong reasons

From my point of view

You believed that you did the right thing

After being told what to do from another

Your actions proved something different

Weakness, selfishness, stubbornness, impatience, rules, and regualtions

So how can there be room for love or friendship

You never fully listened to me

Took me for someone who is beneath you

Money and riches does not make you better then me

But you were able to fool everyone with it

Close their mind's eye shut for a long time

I was not excited nor impressed by anything

You did what you liked

You traded secrets for ill advice

You tried your best day after day to become what I needed

All while trying to light my head on fire

By giving your mom and family the reigns

Expecting me to be obedient and take everything with stride

Take bad behavior and oppression with stride

You failed me and have never been able to make up for that since then

With time I become lost then trapped

Walked around seething with anger, betrayal and confusion

The pain and confusion did not leave me until many years later

It never made me see the full extend of your efforts and good deeds

I was high on hatred

I was toxic and could not come away from that for a long time

But I'm doing better now
I've apologized many times
I am trying to change my ways
You've decided that it's time to leave
Leave if you must I won't stop you
But don't hold old things against me forever
I am remorseful over what I have said and done to you in the past
That is not the person I am now
I'm not happy with the person I have become now either
But that's another story for another day
You act like you don't need me anymore
You have shown me that you can do it all by yourself
You are more then capable of being cold, cruel and even heartless
That is what turned me toxic in the first place
Your good behavior was all fabricated
It was to get something in return I see now
It was not from the heart
You were telling the truth when you said you would not change
I should have believed you
Hope ruined it all for me

I have not been myself for a long time
I did not treat you right
But I can't be heartless like you
My actions will never measure up to that
I was cold to protect my heart
I was selfish because no one thought of me
I was angry because I did not see a proper future with you
Never felt loved or cared for
You were not the one
There was nothing I could do to stop this either
I am still not happy with you
Cuz we are so different
You're all talk
But you cannot set me free
You won't let me leave either
Because you have others to think about
I have made mistakes
I have learnt from most of them
But the end will be a bitter one
For us both
You will forever hold things against me
Lord over your rules, and misery over me

I will always fall short in my own efforts
I will never be able to live my life to the fullest
Only yours

Triggererd

I absolutely hate it when people step out of line
After I have specifically told them I am bothered by
something
They have said or done
Not once but repeatedly
Keep it between us
There is no need
To broadcast my grievances
Or petty dislikes
To the rest of the world

Negative

Why are you so negative a friend asked me one day
I tried to smile and laugh it off but I couldn't
you see, I have always been positive
until one day I understood that it was not the way to
go
I have always remained hopeful when things
remained bleak
I was optimistic when life was grim
I gave out one chance after the other for people to
tell me the truth
respect my boundaries
stay away from bad things
most of the time none of that happened
so what you see now is practicality
I am not negative
I am being level headed now
because being positive just tore away a lot of the good
parts in me
parts i never should given away for others to keep
being positive worn me out
like one's favorite yellow hair ribbon
now frayed and faded
I too feel the same way
so I don't smile as much either
but I hope I don't get frown lines either

About the Author

Farzana Habib

Farzana Habib Is 29. She hopes to one day write children's books and plays, She writes poems and short stories due to her love for words. She loves all things food, traveling, watching movies in her spare time, and sketching. She is currently working on a new novel titled "THE WOMAN IN THE PAINTING"

www.ingramcontent.com/pod-product-compliance
Lightning Source LLC
LaVergne TN
LVHW041635070526
838199LV00052B/3381